THIS COPY OF
BEST BROWNIE JOKES
BELONGS TO

Claire

Donohue

THE BROWNIE J☆O☆K☆E BOOK

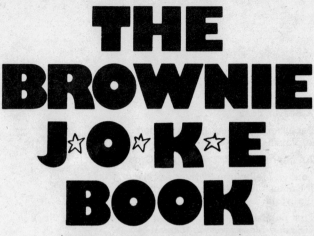

Collected by Brownies
Illustrated by Shelagh McGee

Beaver Books

A Beaver Book

Published by Arrow Books Limited
20 Vauxhall Bridge Road, London SW1V 2SA

An imprint of Random Century Group

London Melbourne Sydney Auckland
Johannesburg and agencies throughout
the world

First published as two volumes, *The Brownie Joke Book*
1983 and *More Brownie Jokes* 1984
Beaver edition 1989
Reprinted 1989

Text © Beaver Books 1983 and 1984
Illustrations © Shelagh McGee 1983 and 1984

Printed and bound in Great Britain by
Courier International Ltd, Tiptree, Essex

ISBN 0 09 965580 2

Foreword

These jokes were sent in by Brownie Guides to their Regional Headquarters and forwarded to the publishing department at Guide Headquarters. Occasionally a very popular joke appeared more than once, in which case it was attributed to the pack who sent it in first . . .

Many thanks to all the Brownies who contributed and happy reading!

FIRST, THE JOKERS.....

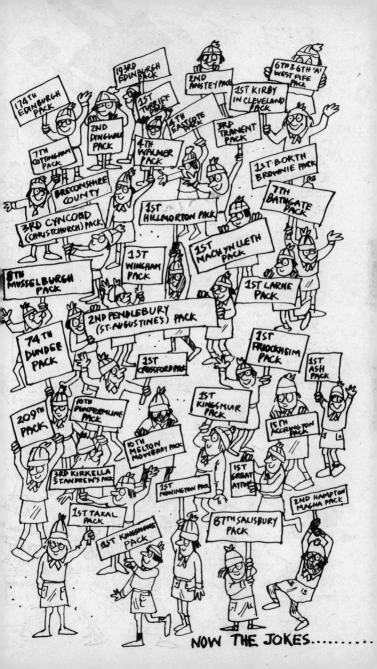

NOW THE JOKES..........

What's big, brown and sometimes white and goes out at night?
Brown Owl.

West Fife Brownies

What is brown all over with red spots?
A Brownie with the measles.

1st Claudy Pack

What do you call a Brownie who wears earmuffs?
You call her anything you like because she can't hear you.

2nd Stokesley Brownie Pack

Why are Brownies dizzy?
Because they are always doing good turns.

Brownies from West Lancashire County

Why did the Brownie throw her watch out of the window?
She wanted to see time fly.

1st Claudy Pack

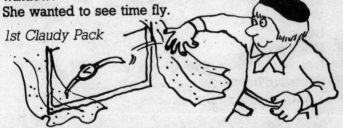

What do you call a Brownie's dad who wears size 12 shoes and does not have a dog?
Big Hughie Douglas.

1st Lesmahagow Brownie Pack

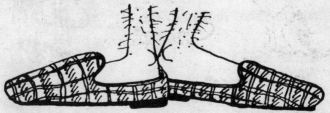

Knock Knock!
Who's there?
Ivor.
Ivor who?
Ivor you let me in through the door or I'll come in through the window.

1st Taxal Pack

Knock Knock!
Who's there?
Frank.
Frank who?
Frankly I don't know.

80th Bradford Brownie Pack

Knock Knock!
Who's there?
Sid.
Sid who?
Sid down and have a cup of tea.

1st Annan Pack

Knock Knock!
Who's there?
Amos.
Amos who?
Amos quito.

1st Hessle Brownie Pack

Knock Knock!
Who's there?
Wendy.
Wendy who?
Wendy red, red robin comes bob, bob, bobbin'
along.

1st Strabane Pack

Knock Knock!
Who's there?
Atch.
Atch who?
Sorry, I didn't know you had a cold.

4th Walmer Pack

Why do polar bears have fur coats?
'Cos they'd look silly in plastic macs.

1st Muckamore 'B' Pack

What kind of fish can't swim?
A dead one.

1st Maybole Pack

What's black, green and white and brown?
A cow with a runny nose in a muddy field.

2nd Pendlebury St Augustine's Pack

How do you catch a squirrel?
Run up a tree and act like a nut.

4th Belfast Pack

What animal eats with its tail?
All animals eat with their tails,
they also sleep with them.

3rd Anerley Pack

Why are goldfish red?
Because the water makes them rusty.

1st Maybole Pack

What animal has two humps and is found at the North Pole?
A lost camel.

7th Crewe Pack

Where does a frog hang his overcoat?
In the croakroom.

1st 'A' Dundonal Pack

What's a big-game hunter?
A chap who loses his way to a football match.

209th Edinburgh Pack

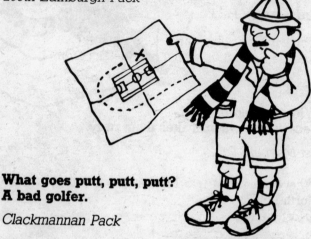

What goes putt, putt, putt?
A bad golfer.

Clackmannan Pack

What's big, green, has four legs and if it fell out of a
tree would kill you?
A snooker table.

Cairw District

Where do snowmen dance?
At a snowball.

1st Wingham Brownie Pack

What ball can you not play with?
An eyeball.

1st Pendlebury St Augustine's Pack

Why can't you play cards in the jungle?
Because there are too many cheetahs around.

2nd Llanishen Pack

Why do jockeys take hay to bed with them?
To feed their nightmares.

1st Spennithorne Brownie Pack

Why didn't they play cards on Noah's Ark?
Because Noah sat on the deck.

Ayrshire South Brownies

Why couldn't the car play football?
Because it only had one boot.

2nd Pendlebury St Augustine's Pack

What's the difference between a sailor and a bargain shopper?
One goes to sail the seas and the other goes to see the sales.

44th Belfast Pack

What did the sea say to the sand?
Nothing, he just waved.

1st Maybole Brownie Pack

What boats remind you of being punished?
Fishing smacks.

17th Rugby Pack

How do fishermen make their nets?
They just take a lot of holes and sew them together.

1st Rhyl Pack

What's the difference between a ton and the ocean?
Wait and see.

3rd Bearsden Pack

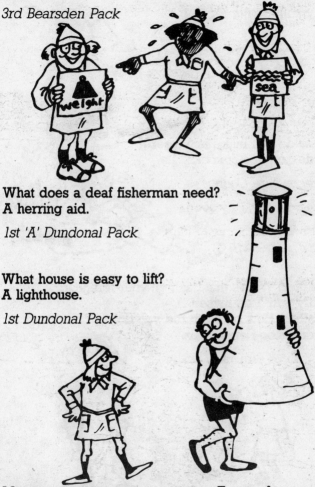

What does a deaf fisherman need?
A herring aid.

1st 'A' Dundonal Pack

What house is easy to lift?
A lighthouse.

1st Dundonal Pack

Mummy, mummy, must we go to France for our holidays?
Be quiet and keep swimming.

7th Crewe Pack

Did you hear about the worm who had Egyptian flu?
Yes, he caught it from his mummy.

Ayrshire South Brownies

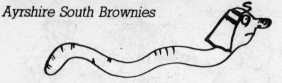

How do you make anti-freeze?
Hide her woolly socks.

Breconshire County

Father: What's that gash on your forehead?
Silly son: I bit myself.
Father: How on earth did you do that?
Son: I stood on a chair.

1st Borth Brownie Pack

Brownie: Mum, I've just got my sewing badge. Can you sew it on for me?

West Lancashire County

Father: What was on the TV today, son?
Son: Same as usual, dad, the lamp and the fish bowl.

3rd Cyncoed (Christchurch) Pack

What did Chief Running Water call his two sons?
Hot and cold.

Clackmannan County

Mary: Grandad, what's a weapon?
Grandad: Something you fight with.
Mary: Is Grandma your weapon then?

1st Crossford Pack

Good news: My mum's just taken me to the zoo.
Bad news: She left me there.

3rd Tranent Pack

Why did the girl tiptoe past the medicine cabinet?
Because she didn't want to wake the sleeping pills.

1st Maybole Brownie Pack

The teacher asked Jimmy, 'Are your parents in, Jimmy?' and he said, 'No, they ain't.' Then the teacher said, 'Where is your grammar?' and Jimmy said, 'In the front room watching telly.'

80th Bradford Brownie Pack

What happened to the kleptomaniac's daughter?
She took after her mother.

Breconshire County

What is the relationship between a doormat and a doorstep?
A step farther.

Clackmannan County

What is nine foot tall, green and wrinkled?
The Incredible Hulk's granny.

Breconshire County

What do porcupines have for dinner?
Prickled onions.

17th Rugby Pack

What do cannibals play at parties?
Swallow my leader.

Ayrshire South Brownies

What does a baby ape sleep in?
An apricot.

4th Walmer Brownie Pack

When is a glass of water sad?
When it has been upset.

1st Wingham Brownie Pack

Why did the orange have to go to the doctor's?
Because it wasn't peeling right.

80th Bradford North Brownie Pack

What fruit appears on every penny?
A date.

4th Walmer Pack

What is vampires' favourite soup?
Scream of tomato.

1st Strabane Pack

What is green and jumps around the garden?
A spring cabbage.

17th Rugby Pack

Knock Knock!
Who's there?
Alison.
Alison who?
Alison the radio.

Breconshire County

Knock Knock!
Who's there?
Tobby.
Tobby who?
Tobby or not Tobby, that is the question.

1st Ash Brownie Pack

Knock Knock!
Who's there?
Senior.
Senior who?
Senior around.

Clackmannan Packs

Knock Knock!
Who's there?
Dishwasher.
Dishwasher who?
Dishwasher way I spoke before I had my false teeth.

1st Hillmorton Brownie Pack

Knock Knock!
Who's there?
Scot.
Scot who?
Scot nothing to do with you.

West Fife Brownies

Knock Knock!
Who's there?
Lionel.
Lionel who?
Lionel get you nowhere.

7th Bathgate Pack

Knock Knock!
Who's there?
Madame.
Madame who?
Madame foot got stuck in the door!

4th Walmer Pack

What does a ghost rooster say?
Spook-a-doodle-doo!

1st Hessle Brownie Pack

Why do little birds in a nest always agree?
Because they don't want to fall out.

1st 'A' Dundonal Pack

Why did the fly dance in the saucer?
It wanted to win the cup.

1st Machynlleth Pack

What do ducks do when they can't fly?
They quack up.

1st Muckamore 'B' Pack

How does a kangaroo cross the Channel?
By Hopper-craft.

1st Hessle Brownie Pack

What has four legs and yellow feathers?
A pair of canaries.

1st Machynlleth Pack

What snake is clever?
An adder.

209th Pack

What key does a skeleton use?
A skeleton key.

1st Strabane Pack

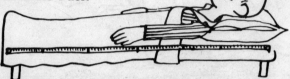

Why do some people take a tape measure to bed with them?
To see how long they sleep.

1st Strabane Pack

How do you use an Egyptian doorbell?
Toot-and-come-in.

1st Wingham Brownie Pack

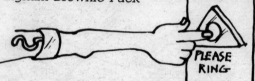

PLEASE RING

Why do you take a pencil to bed with you?
To draw the curtains.

1st Claudy Pack

When is a bucket ill?
When it's a little pail.

Ayrshire South Brownies

What did one wall say to the other wall?
Meet you at the corner.

8th Musselburgh Pack

What sort of lighting did Noah put in his ark?
Flood lighting.

Ayrshire South Brownies

Did you hear about the woman who bought a carpet
that was in mint condition?
It had a hole in the middle.

Brownies from the West Lancashire County

Why did the lady have a packet of Daz on top of her
TV set?
Because she had no aerial.

87th Salisbury Pack

What do you get when you cross an elephant with a kangaroo?
Big holes all over Africa.

1st Nonington Brownie Pack

What's worse than an elephant with a sore trunk?
A centipede with sore feet.

1st 'A' Dundonal Pack

How can you tell when an elephant's been in the fridge?
By the footprints in the butter.

Clacken, Clackmannan County

What did Tarzan say when he saw the elephants coming?
Here come the elephants.

1st 'A' Dundonal Pack

Why can't two elephants go for a swim together?
Because they've only got one pair of trunks between them.

7th Crewe Pack

What is the difference between an Indian elephant and an African elephant?
About 3000 miles.

17th Rugby Pack

Why did the elephant cross the road?
Because the chicken was having a day off.

1st Hessle Brownie Pack

What do you get if you cross an elephant with a mouse?
Large holes in the floorboards.

7th Cottingham (St Mary's) Pack

What did the elephant say to the orange?
Let's play squash.

1st Pendlebury St Augustine's Pack

Why did the elephant cross the road?
To make a trunk call.

1st Strabane Pack

Why don't elephants like penguins?
Because they can't get the paper off.

1st Dundonal Pack

What did the hotel manager say to the elephant
who couldn't pay his bill?
Pack your trunk and clear out.

1st Larne Pack

How do you hide an elephant in a cherry tree?
Paint his toenails red.

7th Crewe Brownie Pack

How does an elephant get down from a tree?
It sits on a leaf and waits for autumn.

1st Strabane Pack

What is most like half an orange?
The other half.

1st Claudy Pack

What is yellow and goes up and down?
A lemon in a lift.

2nd Llanishen Pack

What kind of person is fed up with people?
A cannibal.

17th Rugby Pack

What jam can you not eat?
A traffic jam.

1st Strabane Pack

What kind of dance does a tin opener do?
The Can-Can.

1st Maybole Brownie Pack

What do sea monsters eat?
Fish and ships.

Breconshire County

What bulbs never grow?
Electric light bulbs.

1st Wingham Brownie Pack

What did one chimney say to the other?
You're too small to smoke.

1st 'A' Dundonal Pack

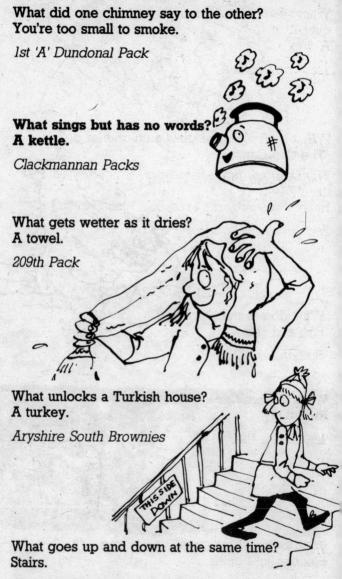

What sings but has no words?
A kettle.

Clackmannan Packs

What gets wetter as it dries?
A towel.

209th Pack

What unlocks a Turkish house?
A turkey.

Aryshire South Brownies

THIS SIDE DOWN

What goes up and down at the same time?
Stairs.

74th Dundee Pack

What often has to be answered but doesn't ask questions?
A doorbell.

1st Borth Pack

What's the difference between a newspaper and the TV?
Have you ever tried swotting a fly with the TV?

2nd Stokesley Brownie Pack

What do you think of a dustbin?
Rubbish!

1st Claudy Pack

Which building has the most stories?
The library.

Clackmannan County

What language do twins speak in Holland?
Double Dutch.

1st Hillmorton Brownie Pack

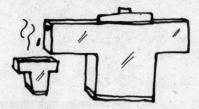

What begins with t, ends with t and has t in it?
A teapot.

1st Rhyl Pack

Sara: You've addressed that letter upside down.
Ruth: That's right – it's going to Australia.

1st Borth Brownie Pack

How do you make a witch itch?
Rub out the W.

Ayrshire South Brownies

What is the end of everything?
The letter G.

Ayrshire South Brownies

When did only three vowels exist?
Before U and I were born.

Ayrshire South Brownies

Which long word has only one letter in it?
An envelope.

1st Claudy Pack

Knock Knock!
Who's there?
Whale meat.
Whale meat who?
Whale meet again.

1st Friockheim Pack

Knock Knock!
Who's there?
Micky.
Micky who?
Micky is lost so that's why I'm knocking.

1st Pendlebury St Augustine's Pack

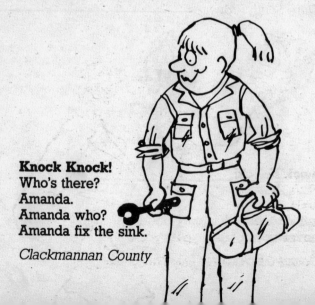

Knock Knock!
Who's there?
Amanda.
Amanda who?
Amanda fix the sink.

Clackmannan County

Knock Knock!
Who's there?
Watson.
Watson who?
Watson the television?

2nd Stokesley Brownie Pack

Knock Knock!
Who's there?
Sheila.
Sheila who?
She loves you yeah, yeah, yeah!

6th and 6th 'A' West Fife Pack

**What is the strongest bird in the world?
The crane.**

1st Crossford Pack

What do you get if you put ducks in a box?
A box of quackers.

17th Rugby Pack

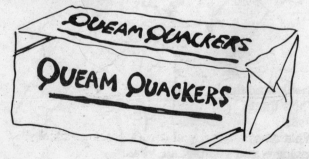

What do you give a sick bird?
Tweetment.

10th Dunfermline Pack

Which bird reminds you of a musician?
A sandpiper.

1st Combs Pack

What do you get if you give a chicken whisky?
Scotch eggs.

8th West Fife Pack

When is a cook cruel?
When she beats eggs and whips cream.

1st Strabane Pack

What's thick, yellow and dangerous?
Shark infested custard.

1st Hillmorton Brownie Pack

What is green and jumps up and down?
A cabbage at a disco.

2nd Pendlebury St Augustine's Pack

What turns without moving?
Milk, when it turns sour.

3rd Bearsden Pack

What kind of biscuit flies?
A plain biscuit.

8th West Fife Pack

Why do Eskimos eat candles?
Because they prefer light meals.

1st Strabane Pack

What's yellow and stupid?
Thick custard.

1st Kingsmuir Pack

What does a skeleton serve his dinner on?
Bone china.

Ayrshire South Brownies

PATIENTS BADGE

Patient: Doctor, doctor, I think I'm going blind.
Doctor: I thought so when you walked in through the window.

15th Accrington Pack

Patient: Doctor, I feel like a pipe sticking out of the back of a car.
Doctor: I thought you looked a bit exhausted.

74th Dundee Pack

Patient: Doctor, doctor, I feel like a clock.
Doctor: Just wait a tick.

8th West Fife Pack

Patient: Doctor, I feel like a bridge.
Doctor: What's come over you?
Patient: Four cars, two lorries and three buses!

55th B 'A' Belfast Pack

Patient: My hair keeps falling out, can you suggest anything to keep it in?
Doctor: How about a carrier bag?

1st 'A' Dundonal Pack

Patient: Doctor, doctor, I feel like a sock.
Doctor: Well, I'll be darned!

Clackmannan Packs

Patient: Doctor, doctor, I can't get to sleep at night.
Doctor: Well, lie at the end of your bed and you'll soon drop off!

1st Claudy Pack

Patient: Doctor, doctor, I feel like an ice cream.
Doctor: So do I, go and buy me one.

1st Taxal Pack

Patient: Doctor, doctor, I feel like a spoon.
Doctor: Well, sit down and don't stir.

1st 'A' Dundonal Pack

Patient: Doctor, doctor, I keep feeling invisible.
Doctor: Who said that?

Doctor: Now, about these headaches . . . have your eyes been checked in the last few months?
Patient: No, doctor, they've always been plain blue.

Patient: Doctor, doctor, I feel like a dustbin.
Doctor: Oh, don't talk rubbish.

What's brown and carries a suitcase?
A handle.

1st Kingsmuir Pack

What holds the moon up?
Moon beams.

Clackmannan County

How do you keep an idiot in suspense?
I'll tell you in the morning.

1st Pendlebury St Augustine's Pack

Why is it against the law to whisper?
Because it isn't aloud.

1st 'A' Dundonal Pack

Why do we sometimes call the Middle Ages the Dark Ages?
Because they have so many knights.

1st Rhyl Pack

What box has no lid?
A pillar box.

1st Wingham Brownie Pack

Why is it useless to send a telegram to Washington?
Because he is dead.

1st Great Ayton

An old man and woman fell down a well. Which one got out first?
The lady – she had a ladder in her tights.

209th Pack

Why is it difficult to keep a secret at the North Pole?
Because your teeth tend to chatter.

1st Hillmorton Brownie Pack

Who invented fire?
Oh, some bright spark.

1st Pendlebury St Augustine's Pack

What is 300 feet high and wobbles?
The trifle tower.

1st Kingsmuir Pack

Did you hear about the fight in the biscuit tin last night?
The Bandit hit the Yo-Yo with a Club, tied him up in Blue Ribbon and got away in a Taxi.

2nd Dingwall Pack

If cakes are 66p how much are upside-down cakes?
99p.

Salford Division

What is green and hairy and drinks out of the wrong side of the glass?
A gooseberry trying to get rid of the hiccups.

1st 'S' Dundonal Pack

What's red and has pips?
A telephone box.

1st Kingsmuir Pack

When is soup musical?
When it's piping hot.

Ayrshire South Brownies

What happened to the man who swallowed a door knob?
It turned his stomach.

Cairw District

What did the astronaut see in his frying pan?
An unidentified frying object.

Clackmannan County

How did the baker get an electric shock?
He stood on a bun and a currant ran up his leg.

1st Kingsmuir Pack

Knock Knock!
Who's there?
Boo.
Boo who?
There's no need to cry, it's only a joke.

1st Pendlebury St Augustine's Pack

Knock Knock!
Who's there?
Luke.
Luke who?
Luke through the keyhole and you'll find out.

2nd Stokesley Brownie Pack

Knock Knock!
Who's there?
Jenny.
Jenny who?
Jenny Wren.

15th Accrington Pack

Knock Knock!
Who's there?
Henrietta.
Henrietta who?
Henrietta banana.

1st Pendlebury St Augustine's Pack

Knock Knock!
Who's there?
Lettuce.
Lettuce who?
Lettuce in and I'll tell you.

2nd Stokesley Brownie Pack

What do you get when you cross a cow with a sheep and a goat?
A Milky Bar Kid.

3rd Pickering Brownie Pack

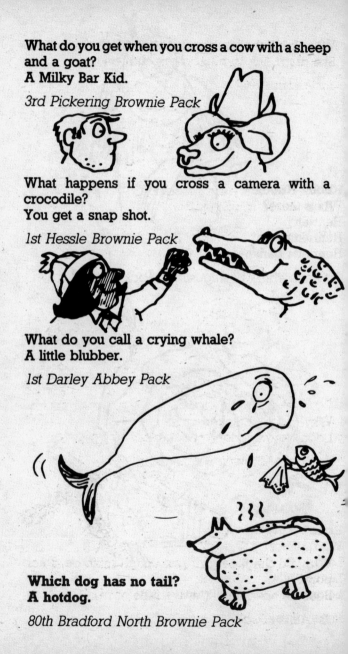

What happens if you cross a camera with a crocodile?
You get a snap shot.

1st Hessle Brownie Pack

What do you call a crying whale?
A little blubber.

1st Darley Abbey Pack

Which dog has no tail?
A hotdog.

80th Bradford North Brownie Pack

Why didn't the lamb make a sound all day?
She didn't like to bleat between meals.

1st Annan Pack

Where do you weigh a whale?
At a whale weigh station.

7th Cottingham (St Mary's) Pack

Why did the chicken cross the road?
I don't know, I don't speak chicken language.

1st Hessle Brownie Pack

Why did the little girl give cough mixture to her pony?
Because she knew it was a little horse.

1st Annan Pack

What has fifty heads but no hair?
A box of matches.

Anne Thompson, 1st Claudy Pack

If a ton of coal comes to £15, what does a ton of firewood come to?
Ashes!

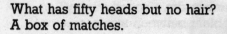

8th Musselburgh Brownie Pack

What is bigger when it is upside down?
The number six.

Ayrshire South Brownies

What lies on the ground, a hundred feet in the air?
A dead centipede.

1st Claudy Pack

If two's company and three's a crowd, what is four and five?
Nine!

Ayrshire South Brownies

How many feet in a yard?
Depends on how many people are standing in it.

Brownies from West Lancashire County

What do you get if you dial 666?

Police, Fire brigade and Ambulance.

1st Great Ayton

Six men were trying to stand under one umbrella.
Why didn't any of them get wet?
Because it wasn't raining.

Brownies from West Lancashire County

What occurs in every minute, twice in a moment,
and yet never in a thousand years?
The letter 'M'.

1st Great Ayton.

What game do crocodiles play?
Snap!

209th Edinburgh Pack

What do they call a camel with three humps?
Humphrey.

1st Machynlleth Pack

What do you give a sick pig?
Oinkment.

1st Crossford Pack

Why are snakes clever?
Because you can't pull their legs.

209th Pack

Why do cows wear bells?
Because they haven't any horns.

1st Combs Pack

Where do cows go on holiday?
Moo York.

1st Theucaston Pack

What did the hen say when she saw a scrambled egg?
There goes my crazy mixed-up kid!

7th Crewe Brownie Pack

What do frogs sit on?
Toadstools.

19th Ilkeston Pack

What is black when clean, and white when dirty?
A blackboard.

1st Kingsmuir Pack

Why did the teacher wear dark glasses?
Because he has such a bright class.

3rd Cyncoed (Christchurch) Pack

Why did silly Billy take a ladder to school?
Because he was going to high school.

17th Rugby Pack

Teacher: When do you like school best?
Pupil: When it's closed.

3rd Cyncoed (Christchurch) Pack

Sally: Would you punish a pupil for something she didn't do?
Teacher: Of course not.
Sally: Good. I haven't done my homework.

17th Rugby Pack

What did the burglar say to the watchmaker?
Sorry to have taken so much of your valuable time.

3rd Cyncoed (Christchurch) Pack

Good news: I got a job as a postman.
Bad news: I got the sack.

1st Lesmahagow Brownie Pack

What happened to the paper shop?
It blew away.

1st Dundonal Pack

Why is it crazy to break into a bank?
Because it's full of coppers.

1st Claudy Pack

What has no hands, no feet, no head, no body but
can still open a door?
The wind.

1st Machynlleth Pack

What room can you bounce?
A ballroom.

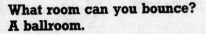

1st Pendlebury St Augustine's Pack

How can you tell if a giant is under your bed?
Your nose touches the ceiling.

Ayrshire South Brownies

Did you hear about the barber who told his customers horror stories?
He made their hair stand on end.

1st Kingsmuir Pack

What does a giant do when he breaks his toe?
He calls a toe truck.

Ayrshire South Brownies

What washing powder does Kojak use?
Bald automatic.

3rd Cyncoed (Christchurch) Pack

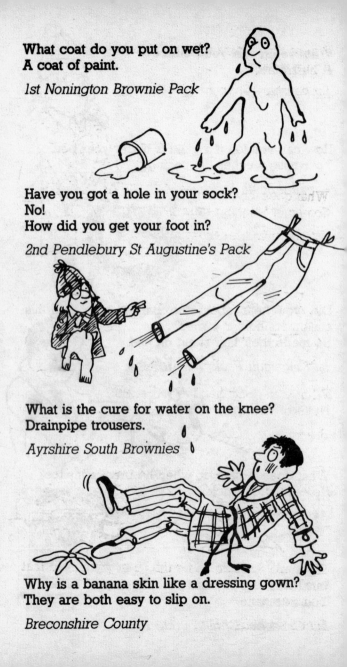

What coat do you put on wet?
A coat of paint.

1st Nonington Brownie Pack

Have you got a hole in your sock?
No!
How did you get your foot in?

2nd Pendlebury St Augustine's Pack

What is the cure for water on the knee?
Drainpipe trousers.

Ayrshire South Brownies

Why is a banana skin like a dressing gown?
They are both easy to slip on.

Breconshire County

Where does Tarzan get his clothes from?
A jungle sale.

Breconshire County

What goes 'ha-ha plop'?
Someone laughing their head off.

1st Spennithorne Brownie Pack

What is the best hand to write with?
Neither. You write with a pen.

Breconshire County

What are the little white things in your head that bite?
Your teeth.

55th B 'A' Belfast Pack

Knock Knock!
Who's there?
Gnome.
Gnome who?
I know you but you don't gno-me.

8th West Fife Pack

Knock Knock!
Who's there?
Merry.
Merry who.
Merry Christmas.

1st Larne Pack

Knock Knock!
Who's there?
Banana.
Banana who?
Knock knock!
Who's there?
Banana
Banana who?
Knock knock!
Who's there?
Orange.
Orange who?
Orange you glad I didn't say banana?

55th B 'A' Belfast Pack

Knock Knock!
Who's there?
Ken.
Ken who?
Ken I come in or do I have to climb through the window?

Clackmannan County

Where does a fish get his money?
From a riverbank.

1st Crossford Pack

What fish makes you think of the sky at night?
A starfish.

7th Ilkeston Pack

Why does a giraffe have such a long neck?
Because its head is so far from its body.

17th Rugby Pack

What goes da-dit-dit croak da-dit-da croak?
A morse toad.

1st Larne Pack

What did the boy octopus sing to the girl octopus?
I want to hold your hand, hand, hand hand, hand, hand, hand, hand!

17th Rugby Pack

Why has a horse got six legs?
It has fore legs at the front and two behind.

4th Walmer Pack

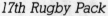

What do you call a camel at the North Pole?
Lost!

8th West Fife Pack

What goes tick, tick, woof, woof?
A watch dog.

17th Rugby Pack

Why don't they grow bananas any longer?
They are long enough already.

80th Bradford Brownie Pack

What did the cabbage say when he knocked on the door?
Lettuce in!

1st Kingsmuir Pack

What has twenty-two legs and goes crunch, crunch, crunch, crunch?
A football team eating crisps.

3rd Cyncoed (Christchurch) Pack

Two spiders were going across a cornflake box.
One started to run and the other said, 'What are you running for?'
'Stupid, it says tear across the dotted line.'

1st 'A' Dundonal Pack

What is yellow and white and travels at 90 mph?
A train driver's egg sandwich.

West Fife Brownies

A cannibal came home one night to find his wife cutting up a small native and a boa constrictor. 'Oh, no,' he said, 'not snake and pigmy pie again!'

2nd Dingwall Pack

What did the ghost say to the barman?
Do you serve spirits in here?

1st Kingsmoore Pack

Little Miss Muffet sat on her tuffet eating her Irish stew. There came a big spider that sat down beside her and she ate that too.

1st Kirby in Cleveland Pack

What do you call a dirty boy crossing the street twice?
A dirty double-crosser.

3rd Bearsden Pack

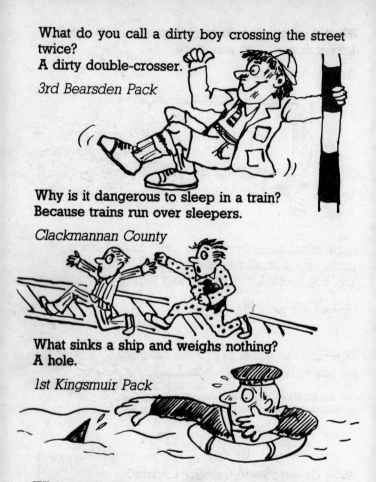

Why is it dangerous to sleep in a train?
Because trains run over sleepers.

Clackmannan County

What sinks a ship and weighs nothing?
A hole.

1st Kingsmuir Pack

What part in the car causes most accidents?
The nut behind the wheel.

1st Borth Pack

Why is a policeman strong?
Because he can hold up traffic.

3rd Kirk Ella 1st Andrews Brownie Pack

What do you call a frozen bike?
An icicle.

1st Strabane Pack

What wobbles and flies?
A jellycopter.

1st Claudy Pack

What did the traffic light say to the man?
Don't look, I'm changing.

1st Hessle Brownie Pack

Why do witches fly on broomsticks?
Because vacuum cleaners are too expensive.

2nd Hampton Magna Pack

Which knot likes going up into space?
An astronaut.

193rd City of Edinburgh Pack

What kind of driver cannot drive a car?
A screwdriver.

1st Claudy Pack

What has one horn and carries milk?
A milk van.

1st Great Ayton

Which bus crossed the ocean?
Columbus.

Clackmannan County

Diana: Please look out and see if our indicators are working.
Lynn: Yes, no, yes, no, yes, no, yes, no, yes ...

1st Muckamore 'B' Pack

What did the man do when he couldn't go down the M6?
He went down the M3 twice.

1st Hessle Brownie Pack

What kind of motorbike would a comedian buy?
A Yama-ha-ha!

8th West Fife Pack

What has four wheels and flies?
A dustcart.

1st Hessle Brownie Pack

What pop group do dogs like best?
Boney M.

1st Spennithorne Brownie Pack

Why did the chicken cross the road?
Because he saw the pelican crossing!

1st Strabane Pack

What goes backwards, and forwards but always stays in the same place?
A rocking horse.

1st Borth Pack

Why did the horse go over the hill?
Because he couldn't go under it.

3rd Pickering Brownie Pack

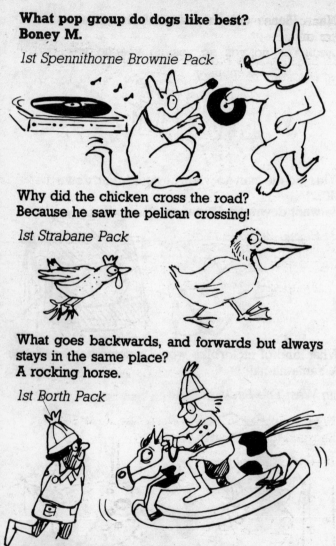

What did the earwig say when he fell over the cliff?
Ear we go!

1st Spennithorne Brownie Pack

What exams do horses take?
Hay levels.

1st Hillmorton Brownie Pack

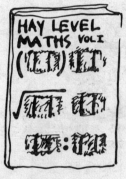

Why do leopards never escape from the zoo?
Because they are always spotted.

Breconshire County

A lady went for a walk and saw a man with a frog in his hand. 'Where are you going with that frog?' she asked.

'I'm taking him to the zoo,' the man replied. Next day the lady saw him again. He was still carrying the frog.

'I thought you took him to the zoo yesterday,' she said.

'I did,' said the man. 'Today I'm taking him to the park.'

4th Eastcote Pack

**What sea bird pants like a train?
A puffin.**

1st Combs Pack

How do you keep a fish from smelling?
Cut off his nose.

1st Strabane Pack

Where do sheep get their wool cut?
At a baa baa's shop.

1st Spennithorne Brownie Pack

First snake: Are we poisonous?
Second snake: Why?
First snake: Because I've just bitten myself.

Brownies from West Lancashire County

Knock Knock!
Who's there?
Angus.
Angus who?
Angus ma coat up please?

2nd Pendlebury St Augustine's Pack

Knock Knock!
Who's there?
Owl.
Owl who?
Owl cry if you don't let me in.

4th Eastcote Pack

Knock Knock!
Who's there?
Dishes.
Dishes who?
Dishes the Police, open up!

8th West Fife Pack

Knock Knock!
Who's there?
Lemmy.
Lemmy who?
Lemmy in at once!

17th Rugby Pack

Knock Knock!
Who's there?
J.R.
J.R. who?
J.R. coming to take you away, ha-ha!

1st Strabane Pack

What runs round the forest making animals yawn?
A wild boar.

West Fife Brownies

What ant is the youngest?
An infant.

West Fife Brownies

What is grey, has wheels and squeaks?
A mouse on roller skates.

Breconshire County

What do you get when you pour hot tea down a rabbit hole?
Hot cross buns.

6th and 6th 'A' West Fife Pack

Why do bees hum?
Because they don't know the words.

55th B 'A' Belfast Pack

Why did the ant dance on top of the jam jar?
Because it said 'Twist to open'.

1st Claudy Pack

How does an octopus go into battle?
Fully armed.

1st Lesmahagow Brownie Pack

What kind of cat do you find in the library?
A catalogue.

17th Rugby Pack

Where do fleas race together?
In a flea-legged race.

Breconshire County

**What is a foreign ant?
Important.**

17th Rugby Pack

**What do you get if you cross a sheep dog with a jelly?
Collie-wobbles.**

Breconshire County

**How does a cat go down the M1?
Mieowwwwwwwwwwww!**

87th Salisbury Pack

Diner: Waiter, what is wrong with these eggs?
Waiter: I don't know, sir, I only laid the table.

3rd Cyncoed (Christchurch) Pack

Diner: Waiter, waiter, will the pancakes be long?
Waiter: No, sir, round.

1st Claudy Pack

Customer: Waiter, have you got frog's legs?
Waiter: No, sir, I always walk like this.

6th and 6th 'A' West Fife Pack

Diner: Why is this chop so tough?
Waiter: Well, sir, it's a karate chop.

1st Rhyl Pack

Man: Waiter, there's a button in my soup!
Waiter: I expect it fell off, sir, when the salad was dressing.

1st Ash Brownie Pack

What do bees do with honey?
Cell it.

1st Turriff Pack

What trees have neither leaves nor bark?
Shoe trees.

Salford Division

What do you call two rows of cabbages?
A dual cabbage way.

3rd Pickering Brownie Pack

Why couldn't the orange get up the hill?
Because it hadn't enough juice.

3rd Pickering Brownie Pack

What's green and runs up the wall?
A runner bean

1st Machynlleth Pack

What did one strawberry say to the other strawberry?
Between you and me, we shouldn't have got into this jam.

1st Pendlebury St Augustine's Pack

What is yellow and points north?
A magnetic banana.

Breconshire County

What is green and hairy and goes up and down?
A gooseberry in a lift.

1st Claudy Pack

What's brown, hairy and wears sunglasses?
A coconut on holiday.

West Fife Brownies

What is more invisible than the Invisible Man?
His shadow.

Ayrshire South Brownies

When do broken bones become useful?
When they begin to knit.

1st 'A' Dundonal Pack

Why does the king wear red, white and blue braces?
To keep his trousers up.

174th City of Edinburgh Pack

What has a bottom at its top?
A leg.

Breconshire County

What do you get hanging from a tree?
Sore arms.

Breconshire County

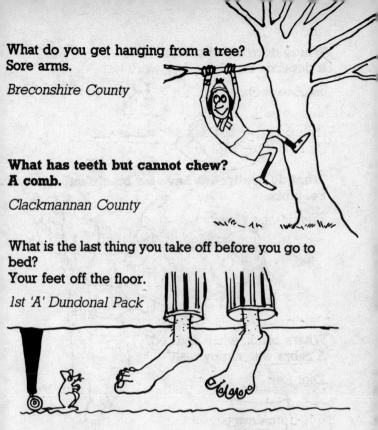

What has teeth but cannot chew?
A comb.

Clackmannan County

What is the last thing you take off before you go to bed?
Your feet off the floor.

1st 'A' Dundonal Pack

What tree does everyone carry in their hand?
A palm.

3rd Bearsden Pack

What did the water say to the bathtub?
I'll give you a ring on Saturday night.

Ayrshire South Brownies

Where do you find rabbits?
It depends on where they were lost.

1st Annan Pack

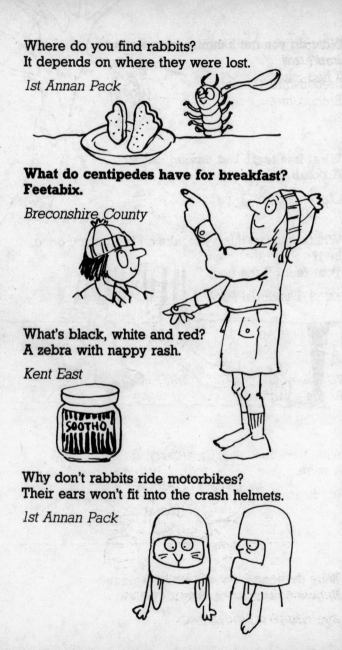

**What do centipedes have for breakfast?
Feetabix.**

Breconshire County

What's black, white and red?
A zebra with nappy rash.

Kent East

Why don't rabbits ride motorbikes?
Their ears won't fit into the crash helmets.

1st Annan Pack

Did you hear about the cat who swallowed a ball of wool?
It had mittens.

Breconshire County

What ant is the biggest?
A giant.

West Fife Brownies

Where would you find giant snails?
At the end of his fingers, of course.

2nd Anstey Pack

Why do bees have sticky hair?
Because they have honey combs.

2nd Hampton Magna Pack

MORE
BROWNIE
JOKES

Collected by Brownies

Illustrated by Shelagh McGee

First Brownie: Shall I tell you the one about the butter?
Second Brownie: Butter not, I might spread it.

80th Bradford Pack

Why did the Brownie put her bed in the fireplace?
Because she wanted to sleep like a log.

1st Muckamore Pack

First Brownie: What is the 25th letter of the alphabet?
Second Brownie: Y.
First Brownie: Because I asked you.

80th Bradford Brownie Pack

First Brownie: Did you hear about the plastic surgeon who stood by the fire?
Second Brownie: No.
First Brownie: He melted.

West Fife Brownies

Why did the Brownie place a loaf of bread in her comic?
Because she liked crumby jokes.

8th West Fife Pack

What has eyes but cannot see?
A potato.

West Fife Brownies

How many cowboys are there in a tin of tomatoes?
None – they're all redskins.

6th and 6thA West Fife Pack

Why did the orange stop in the middle of the road?
Because it ran out of juice.

15th Accrington Pack

There were two eggs in a pan. One egg said to the other: 'It's hot in here.' The other said, 'Wait till you get outside. They'll bash your head in!'

Breconshire County Pack

First Brownie: Have you heard the story of the three eggs?
Second Brownie: No.
First Brownie: Two bad.

3rd Pickering Brownie Pack

Why did the egg go into the jungle?
Because it was an eggsplorer.

1st Annan Brownie Pack

Why did the tomato run?
To ketchup.

3rd Pickering Pack

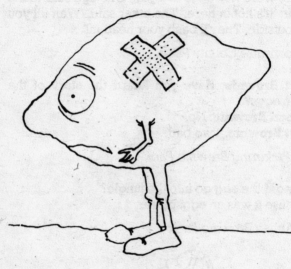

What do you give a hurt lemon?
Lemonade, of course.

1st Friockheim Pack

What is small, green and does good turns?
A cub sprout.

1st Muckamore Pack

What sort of shoes are made out of banana skins?
Slippers.

Salford Division

What are egg shells used for?
To keep eggs together.

1st Larne Pack

What runs round the garden at 100 mph?
A runner bean.

1st Spennithorne Pack

Knock knock
Who's there?
Europe.
Europe who?
Europe early.

2nd Pendlebury St Augustine's Pack

Knock knock
Who's there?
Ivor.
Ivor who?
Ivor a good mind not to tell you.

1st Strabane Pack

Knock knock
Who's there?
Egbert.
Egbert who?
Egbert no bacon.

1st Spennithorne Brownie Pack

Knock knock
who's there?
Alick.
Alick who?
Alick my lollipop.

2nd Stokesley Brownie Pack

What is grey, has four legs and a trunk?
A mouse on holiday.

87th Salisbury Pack

Once a rabbit felt hungry so he went to the pub and asked if they sold things to eat. The barman replied: 'Toasties: Ham or cheese and tomato.'
The rabbit had a ham toastie and a pint of beer. When he had eaten this he asked for a cheese and tomato toastie. When the rabbit finished this he fell down dead.
That evening the ghost of the rabbit appeared. The barman asked him what he had died of, and the rabbit replied: 'Mixin Ma Toasties'.

West Lancashire County

Where do hamsters come from?
Hamsterdam.

4th Eastcote Pack

What animal is found on every legal document?
A seal.

Salford Division

What do apes cook their lunch on?
Gorillas.

6th and 6thA West Fife Pack

What are assets?
Little donkeys.

Clackmannan Packs

What did the kangaroo say when its baby went missing?
Someone's picked my pocket!

74th Dundee Pack

Why did the tortoise beat the hare?
Because there is nothing faster than Shell.

55th 'A' Belfast Pack

What goes to sleep with its shoes on?
A horse.

2nd Dingwall Pack

What did the horse say when he got to the end of his bag?
That's the last straw.

Ayrshire South Brownies

Where do horses go when they are sick?
Horsepital.

55th 'A' Belfast Pack

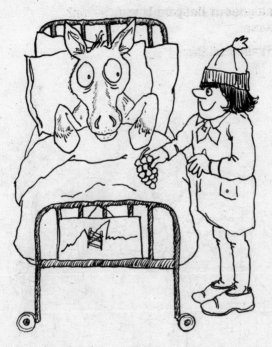

Why did the farmer call his pig Ink?
Because it kept running out of its pen.

1st Claudy Pack

What lion can't roar?
A dandelion.

1st Strabane Pack

What has sixty keys but can't open any doors?
A piano.

87th Salisbury Pack

What has legs but cannot walk?
A chair.

4th Walmer Pack

Why is a piano like an eye?
Because both are closed when their lids are down.

17th Rugby Pack

What did the bubble gum say to the carpet?
I'm stuck on you.

West Fife Brownies

If a blue house is made of blue bricks and a red house is made of red bricks and a yellow house is made of yellow bricks, what is a green house made of?
Glass.

1st Muckamore 'B' Pack

What pie can fly?
A magpie.

1st Annan Pack

Sarah: Do you know you have a hot-dog behind your ear?
Lynette: Oh no! I must have eaten my pencil for lunch.

1st Muckamore 'B' Pack

What did the mayonnaise say to the refrigerator?
Close the door – I'm dressing.

Kent East Pack

What do pixies have for tea?
Fairy cakes.

1st Claudy Pack

What's yellow, soft and goes round and round?
A long-playing omelette.

1st Annan Pack

What is abundance?
A disco for cakes.

10th Dunfermline Pack

What type of thief steals meat?
A hamburglar.

Kent East Brownies

Diner: Waiter, what soup is this?
Waiter: It's bean soup.
Diner: I don't care what it's been, what is it now?

1st Borth Pack

Diner: Waiter, this coffee is terrible – it tastes like earth.
Waiter: Yes sir, it was ground yesterday.

3rd Cyncoed Pack

What did the cannibal say when his friend was late for supper?
Everyone's eaten.

87th Salisbury Pack

How do you make gold soup?
With twenty two carrots.

1st Annan Pack

If bricks make walls, what do walls make?
Ice cream.

8th Fife Pack

What stays hot in the fridge?
Mustard.

3rd Pickering Brownie Pack

Knock knock.
Who's there?
Cook.
Cook who?
That's the first one I've heard this year.

Pixies of 2nd Leyburn Pack

Knock knock
Who's there?
Tarmac.
Tarmac who?
Tarmac kangeroo down sport!

West Fife Brownies

Knock knock
Who's there?
Witches.
Witches who?
Witches the way to go home?

193rd City of Edinburgh Pack

Knock knock
Who's there?
Jaws.
Jaws who?
Jaws one cornetto. . . .

6th and 6thA West Fife Pack

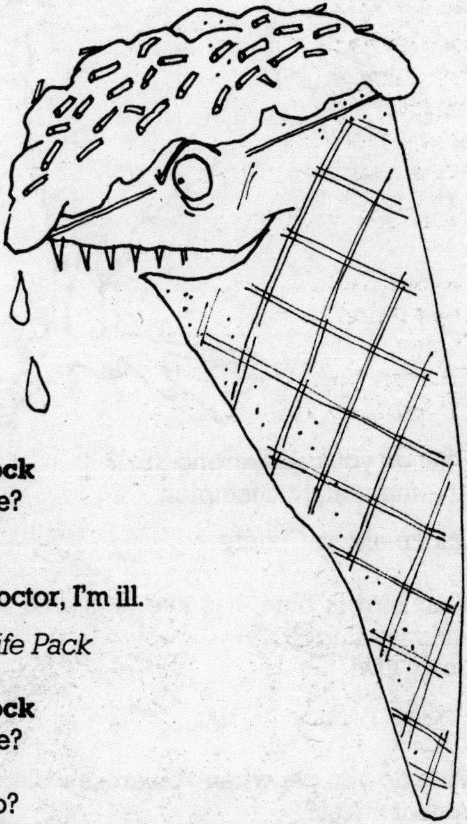

Knock knock
Who's there?
Colin.
Colin who?
Colin the doctor, I'm ill.

8th West Fife Pack

Knock knock
Who's there?
Teresa.
Teresa who?
Teresa green.

80th Bradford North Pack

What do you call a strong bird?
A featherweight champion.

Clackmannan County

What bird is blue, has two legs, and is a hoot at pack meetings?
Brown Owl.

1st Claudy Pack

What do you get when you cross a chicken with a cement mixer?
A layer of concrete.

1st Rhyl Pack

Why did the chicken leave home?
Because it was tired of being cooped up

1st Kingsmuir Brownie Pack

What kind of crow never flies?
A scarecrow.

Stockport County Packs

When is a turkey like a ghost?
When it's a goblin.

1st Turiff Pack

What do you get if you cross an owl with a skunk?
A bird that smells but doesn't give a hoot.

Ayrshire South Brownies

What do you call an elephant that flies?
A jumbo jet.

1st Larne Pack

Can elephants jump higher than lamp-posts?
Yes. Lamp-posts can't jump.

1st Larne Pack

What time is it when a load of elephants sit on your fence?
Time to get a new fence.

7th Crewe Pack

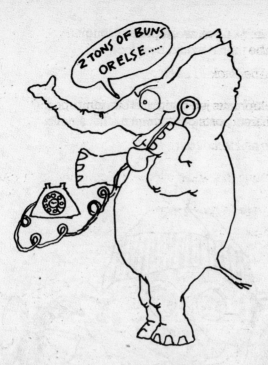

Why has an elephant got Big Ears?
Because Noddy won't pay the ransom.

1st Pendlebury St Augustine's Pack

Why is an elephant large, grey and wrinkled?
Because if it was small, white and round it would be an aspirin.

3rd Cyncoed Pack

What's grey and white and red all over?
An embarrassed elephant.

1st Larne Pack

Why isn't a nose twelve inches long?
Because then it would be a foot.

1st 'A' Dundonald Pack

What did one eye say to the other?
There's something between us that smells.

Pixies of 2nd Leyburn Pack

What has four legs but only one foot?
A bed.

1st Machynlleth Pack

Why do people laugh up their sleeves?
Because that's where their funny bone is.

1st Muckamore 'B' Pack

Why are tall people lazy?
Because they lie longer in bed.

193rd Edinburgh Pack

How high do people usually stand?
Over two feet.

17th Rugby Pack

Why did mummy flea look so sad?
'Cos all her children went to the dogs.

1st Muckamore 'B' Pack

When a fly from one side of the room and a flea from the other meet, what is the time when they pass?
Fly past flea.

1st Rhyl Pack

When insects take a trip, how do they travel?
In a buggy.

1st Turiff Pack

Why wouldn't they let the butterfly into the ball?
Because it was a moth ball.

4th Eastcote Pack

What goes 99 thump, 99 thump, 99 thump?
A centipede with a wooden leg.

Salford Division

Where do tadpoles change into frogs?
In the croakroom.

1st Claudy Pack

What happened to the snake with a cold?
She adder viper nose.

Ayrshire South Brownies

How do you start a flea race?
One, two, flea, go!

3rd Cyncoed Pack

What's worse than a snake with sore ribs?
A centipede with athlete's foot.

1st Turiff Pack

What did the mother glow-worm say to her son's teacher?
Isn't he bright for his age?

1st Turiff Pack

What do frogs drink?
Croaka Cola.

55th B 'A' Belfast Pack

What goes zzub zzub?
A bee flying backwards.

1st Strabane Pack

ZZUB ZZUB

BUZZ BUZZ

What did one ghost say to the other?
Spook for yourself.

1st Annan Pack

What kind of fur do you get from a werewolf?
As fur as you can.

Ayrshire South Pack

What does Dracula have for breakfast?
Ready neck.

1st Larne Pack

What do they call Dracula?
A pain in the neck.

1st Annan Pack

What do you call a space magician?
A flying saucerer.

1st Annan Pack

Why is a vampire easy to feed?
Because he eats necks to nothing.

1st Froickheim Pack

What do ghosts call their navy?
Ghost Guards.

1st Larne Pack

Where does Dracula get his jokes from?
His crypt writer.

44th Belfast Pack

Who snoops around graveyards with a magnifying glass?
Sherlock Bones.

Breconshire County Pack

Knock knock
Who's there?
Tick.
Tick who?
Tick 'em up, I'm a tongue-tied cowboy.

Clackmannan County Pack

Knock knock
Who's there?
Justin.
Justin who?
Justin time for the party!

1st Pendlebury St Augustine's Pack

What ring is square?
A boxing ring.

8th West Fife Pack

Does this pen write under water?
Yes, and lots of other words too.

4th Walmer Pack

What has an eye but cannot see?
A needle.

1st Annan Pack

What's blue and wears a red scarf?
A freezing snowman.

1st Machynlleth Pack

How many balls of string would it take to reach from the earth to the moon?
Only one if it was long enough.

1st Machynlleth Pack

What did the envelope say to the stamp?
Stick with me and we'll go places.

1st Muckamore Pack

What did the puddle say to the rain?
Drop in again sometime.

1st Annan Pack

What goes round a field but doesn't move.
A hedge.

74th Dundee Pack

When is water like fat?
When it's dripping.

Salford Division

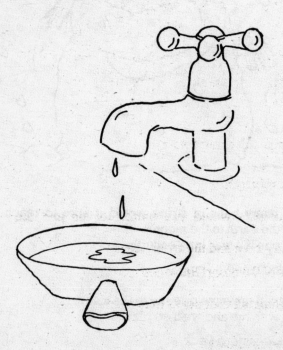

What runs but cannot walk?
Water.

1st Crossford Pack

What colours would you paint the sun and the wind?
The sun – rose and the wind – blue.

County of Stockport Brownies

What often falls but never gets hurt?
Rain.

7th Ilkeston Pack

What do you call a dentist surgery?
A filling station.

West Fife Brownies

What magazines do gardeners read?
The Weeders Digest.

Breconshire County Pack

What is the only business you can see through?
Window cleaning.

209th Edinburgh Pack

What do you call a Scottish cloakroom attendant?
Angus Coatup.

44th Belfast Pack

What do you call an Indian cloakroom attendant?
Mahatma Coat.

44th Belfast Pack

Why was the farmer cross?
Someone trod on his corn.

Clackmannan County Brownies

What did the fireman's wife find on Christmas day?
A ladder in her stocking.

1st Dunfermline Pack

A sheriff rode into town one day and asked the people, 'Have you seen a cowboy wearing a paper hat and shirt?'
'No,' they replied, 'what's he wanted for?'
'Rustlin'.'

1st 'A' Dundonald Pack

How do fish count?
On fish fingers.

1st Kingsmuir Pack

How are the fish today, angler?
I don't know. I've dropped a line but they haven't answered yet.

Ayrshire South Brownies

What goes up a river at 80 mph?
A motor pike.

19th Ilkeston Pack

Why did the biscuit cry?
Because its mother had been a wafer so long.

1st Crossford Pack

What is the best thing to put in a tart?
Teeth.

1st Machynlleth Pack

Diner: This lobster has only one claw.
Waiter: He must have lost one in a fight, sir.
Diner: In that case, I'll have the winner.

3rd Cyncoed Pack

How do you start a pudding race?
Sa-go.

Clackmannan Packs

Judge: Order, order in court!
Criminal: I'll have fish and chips, two rounds of toast, and a pot of tea please.

Breconshire County Pack

Daughter: But Mum, I don't like cheese with holes.
Mother: Well eat the cheese, and leave the holes on the side of your plate.

1st Strabane Pack

Where do fish learn to play?
At plaice school.

1st Dundonald Pack

What is a beetroot?
A potato with very high blood pressure.

1st Pendlebury St Augustine's Pack

What swings from cake to cake?
Tarzipan.

8th West Fife Pack

Why did the tomato blush?
Because he saw the salad dressing.

3rd Bearsden Pack

Why are eggs like bricks?
Because they have to be laid.

80th Bradford North Pack

Patient: Doctor, doctor can you help me out?
Doctor: Certainly, which way did you come in?

Clackmannan Packs

A boy with an elephant on his head went to see a doctor. The doctor said, 'Wow, you really need help.'
'You said it,' the elephant cried, 'get this kid off my foot!'

1st Borth Pack

Patient: Will my chickenpox be better next week?
Doctor: I don't like making rash promises.

1st Broth Pack

Patient: Doctor, doctor, I feel like a bell.
Doctor: Give me a ring when you feel better.

2nd Pendlebury Pack

Patient: Doctor, doctor, I keep seeing pink and blue elephants.
Doctor: Have you seen a psychiatrist?
Patient: No, only pink and blue elephants.

Breconshire County

Patient: Doctor, doctor, I feel like a pair of curtains.
Doctor: Pull yourself together.

2nd Pendlebury St Augustine's Pack

Patient: Doctor, doctor, my nose keeps running. I don't know what to do.
Doctor: Well stick your foot out in front of you and trip it up.

26th Bradford North Pack

Patient: Doctor, doctor, I feel like a window.
Doctor: Just tell me where your pane is.

8th West Fife Pack

Patient: Doctor, doctor, I feel like a snooker ball.
Doctor: Be patient and go to the end of the cue.

1st 'A' Dundonald Pack

Patient: Doctor, doctor, I feel like a pack of cards.
Doctor: Well, don't shuffle about, I'll deal with you later.

1st Dundonald Pack

Patient: Doctor, doctor, everyone ignores me.
Doctor: Next please!

Breconshire County

Teacher: Can you tell me something about the great chemists of the seventeenth century?
Pupil: Yes sir – they're all dead.

1st Kingsmuir Pack

Teacher: Julie, why are you crawling?
Julie: But miss, you said I must never walk in late.

1st Crossford Pack

Telephone conversation:
Teacher: You say Tommy has a cold and can't come to school – who am I speaking to?
Tommy: This is my father.

1st Broth Brownie Pack

Teacher: What family does the rhinoceros belong to?
Pupil: I don't know miss, nobody in our street has one.

1st Rhyl Pack

What do elves do after school?
Gnome work.

1st Machynlleth Pack

What is the difference between a train minder and a teacher?
One minds the train and the other trains the mind.

2nd Llanishen Pack

Did you hear about the cross-eyed teacher?
She couldn't control her pupils.

1st Annan Pack

First Boy: Do you think the teacher likes you?
Second Boy: Yes, she puts kisses all over my book.

1st Crossford Pack

How much is 5Q + 5Q?
10Q.
You're welcome!

1st Pendlebury St Augustine's Pack

What did the man say when he found out he was going bald?
Hair today, gone tomorrow.

8th West Fife Pack

What did the hat say to the scarf?
I'll go on ahead, you hang around.

8th Melton Mowbray Pack

What did the wig say to the head?
I've got you covered.

1st Annan Pack

What did they give to the man who invented door knockers?
The Nobel Prize.

6th and 6th 'A' West Fife Pack

Who was the fastest runner in history?
Adam. He was the first in the human race.

8th West Fife Pack

Where are English kings crowned?
On their heads.

1st Annan Pack

First Brownie: Do you know the difference between a post-box and an elephant with gout?
Second Brownie: No, I don't.
First Brownie: I'm not sending you to post any letters.

1st Great Ayton Pack

When do elephants have eight feet.
When there are two of them.

4th Eastcote Pack

What's the difference between an elephant and a slice of bread?
Have you ever tried dipping an elephant in an egg?

1st Crewe Pack

What do you get if you cross a fish with an elephant?
Swimming trunks.

2nd Llanishen Pack

Why does an elephant paint his feet yellow?
So he can hide upside down in custard.

1st Hessle Pack

What's black and dangerous and lives up a tree?
A crow with a sub-machine gun.

Clackmannan County Packs

**What do you get when you cross a lawn-mower
with a budgie?**
Shredded tweet.

8th Musselburgh Pack

Why is the sky so high?
So the birds don't bump their heads.

Ayrshire South Brownies

What bird has no beak?
A ladybird.

Stockport County Brownies

What goes black and white, black and white, black and white?
A penguin rolling downhill.

4th Eastcote Pack

When is a bus not a bus?
When it turns into a street.

1st Airlie and Ruthuen Pack

Lady: Call me a taxi my good man.
Man: Certainly madam, 'You are a taxi.'

1st Spennithorne Brownie Pack

What was the tortoise doing on the M1?
About 2 mph.

Cairw District Pack

Why do you rest your bike against the wall?
Because it is two-tyred.

1st Darley Abbey Pack

First man: My car had wooden wheels, wooden seats, and a wooden engine.
Second man: No wonder it wooden go!

1st Nonington Brownie Pack

What is the best thing to take if you are run over?
The number of the car that hit you!

17th Rugby Pack

What is black and white and highly dangerous?
A vicar on a skateboard.

19th Ilkeston Pack

How do you get to Tenby?
1b, 2b, 3b, 4b, 5b, 6b, 7b, 8b, 9b, 10b!

2nd Llanishen Pack

Knock knock
Who's there?
Bernadette.
Bernadette who?
Bernadette all my dinner and I'm starving!

7th Bathgate Pack

Will you remember me tomorrow? (yes)
Will you remember me in a week? (yes)
Will you remember me in a month? (yes)
Will you remember me in a year? (yes)
Knock knock
Who's there?
Forgotten me already?

15th Accrington Pack

Knock knock
Who's there?
Doctor.
Doctor who?
How did you guess?

1st Claudy Pack

Knock knock
Who's there?
Isabelle.
Isabelle who?
Isabelle necessary on a bicycle?

15th Accrington Pack

Knock knock
Who's there?
Senior.
Senior who?
Senior so nosy, I'm not going to tell you.

8th West Fife Pack

Knock knock
Who's there?
Cow go.
Cow go who?
Cow go moo, not who!

44th Belfast Pack

What is the best belt to wear on a boat?
A life-belt.

1st Combs Pack

Lady swimming: Help, help! There's a shark!
Boy in boat: Don't worry miss, it's a maneater.

1st Spennithorne Brownie Pack

What is the nicest ship of all?
Friendship.

7th Crewe Pack

Why does the ocean roar?
You would too if you had lobsters in your bed.

3rd Bearsden Pack

What horse doesn't wear a saddle?
A seahorse.

Ayrshire South Brownies

When is a black dog not a black dog?
When it's a greyhound.

Ayrshire South Brownies

What's worse than raining cats and dogs?
Hailing taxis.

1st Annan Pack

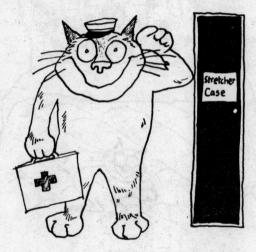

What do you call a cat who wants to join the ambulance service?
A first aid kit.

1st Rhyl Pack

If your cat ate a lemon, what would she become?
A sourpuss.

1st Turiff Pack

Why did the boy call his pet dog Smithy?
Because every time somebody called, the dog made a bolt for the door.

11th Arbroath Pack

Why did the man buy a black and white dog?
He thought the licence would be cheaper.

1st Claudy Pack

If a dog loses his tail where does he get another?
From the re-tail shop.

Salford Division

Why does a dog bark?
Because if it meowed it would be a cat.

1st Larne Pack

How many jelly babies can you fit into an empty jar?
None – or the jar wouldn't be empty, would it?

1st Pendlebury St Augustine's Pack

Why did the jelly wobble?
Because it saw the milk shake.

7th Crewe Pack

What's the best slimming exercise?
Shaking your head when someone offers you food.

209th Edinburgh Pack

What sugar sings?
Icing sugar.

1st Tlaiby Pack

Why is the letter K like flour?
You can't make cake without it.

1st Annan Pack

What do jelly babies wear on their feet?
Gum boots.

1st Annan Pack

What did the bull say to the cow?
When I fall in love, it will be for heifer.

Clackmannan County Pack

What do you get if you catch a sheep in the rain?
A wet blanket.

4th Eastcote Pack

Why has a milking chair only three legs.
Because the cow has the udder.

2nd Chinley Pack

How is the 'g' in August like a shepherd?
Because it is surrounded by u's (ewes).

1st Larne Pack

What do you call a bull asleep on the ground?
A bulldozer.

Clackmannan Pack

What do you call a cow eating grass?
A lawn-mooer.

Clackmannan County

Why did the cowslip?
Because she saw the bullrush.

1st Kirby in Cleveland Pack

Why is the letter V like an angry bull?
Because it comes after U.

Ayrshire South Brownies

What did the goat say when he ate a reel of film?
The book was better.

1st Turiff Pack

Why did the farmer feed his cow money?
Because he wanted rich milk.

8th West Fife Pack

How do you milk a hedgehog?
Very carefully.

3rd Anerley Pack

Why is grass dangerous?
Because it's full of blades.

87th Salisbury Pack

What do elephants play in the back of mini cars?
Squash.

5th Barking Pack

What breaks through a wall and mopes?
The incredible sulk!

7th Plumstead Pack

I say, I say, I say, what did one candle say to the other candle?
I don't know, what did one candle say to the other candle?
Are you going out tonight?

2nd Pendlebury St Augustine's Pack

Who is the boss of the hankies?
The Hankie Chief.

West Ham Brownies

Why was Cinderella dropped from the hockey team?
She kept running away from the ball.

19th Ilkeston Pack

What did Batman give Robin for his supper?
A raw worm.

1st Machynlleth Pack

Once there was a man who sat up all night wondering where on earth the sun had gone to. Next morning it dawned on him.

55th B 'A' Belfast Pack

What always walks with its head on the floor? A nail in your shoe.

1st Annan Pack

When does the day seem short? When there's a morning mist.

1st Darley Abbey Pack

Which kind of bow is it impossible to tie?
A rainbow.

1st Claudy Pack

What can fall on the water and not get wet?
A shadow.

Clackmannan County Pack

When will a net hold water?
When the water is frozen to ice.

8th West Fife Pack

Why did the policeman cry?
Because he couldn't take his Panda to bed.

3rd Pickering Brownie Pack

What would come up if you dug a hole in the road?
A policeman.

7th Bathgate Pack

What do you get when you cross a bald-headed
detective with a camera?
A Kojak instamatic.

Breconshire County Pack

Who chews gum and chases spies?
Bubble-oh-Seven.

West Fife Brownies

Who was the first underwater spy?
James Pond.

Breconshire County Pack

Why did the robber take a bath?
So he could make a clean getaway.

19th Ilkeston Pack

What did the German policeman say to his chest?
You are under a vest!

St James Brownie Pack

What goes up but never comes down?
Your age.

3rd Pickering Brownie Pack

Why did the man climb up the chandelier?
He was a light sleeper.

1st Annan Pack

How do you make a band stand?
Take away their seats.

1st Larne Pack

Why did the Scotsman break a window?
Because he wanted to see glass go.

1st Dundonald Pack

Why are you always tired on April Fools Day?
Because you have just had a March of 31 days.

1st Combs Pack

What question can never be answered by yes?
Are you asleep?

17th Rugby Pack

What happened to the man who couldn't tell the difference between putty and porridge?
His windows fell out.

1st Larne Pack

What goes right up to the door, but never comes inside?
A doorstep.

1st Claudy Pack

Why did the tap run away?
Because it saw the kitchen sink

2nd Pendlebury St Augustine's Pack

When is a door not a door?
When it's a jar.

4th Walmer Pack

Sharon: Did you know that someone invented something that lets you look through walls?
Cathy: No.
Sharon: It's called a window.

1st Muckamore 'B' Pack

How do you keep a house warm?
Paint it with two coats.

West Fife Brownies

What is bought by the yard and worn by the feet?
A carpet.

4th Kirriemuir Pack

Knock knock
Who's there?
You're a lady.
You're a lady who?
Hey, I didn't know you could yodel.

1st Great Ayton Pack

Knock knock
Who's there?
Major.
Major who?
Major answer.

Kent East Brownies

Knock knock
Who's there?
Wilma.
Wilma who?
Wilma tea be ready soon?

West Fife Brownies

Knock knock
Who's there?
Isaac.
Isaac who?
Isaac coming in!

1st Darley Abbey Pack

Knock knock
who's there?
Sam.
Sam who?
Sam one just knocked at the door.
3rd Tranent Pack

Why are carrots good for your eyes?
Well, have you ever seen a rabbit with glasses?

1st Annan Pack

Why do giraffes have such small appetites?
Because a little goes a long way.

1st Maybole Pack

If a husky dog can stand the lowest temperatures, which dog can stand the highest?
A hot dog.

193rd Edinburgh Pack

How do you get a skunk to stop smelling?
Hold his nose.

West Fife Brownies

What is white, furry and smells of peppermint?
A Polo bear.

1st Maybole Pack

Father bear: Who's been eating my porridge?
Baby bear: And who's been eating my porridge?
Mother bear: Belt-up, I haven't made it yet!

1st Kingsmuir Pack

What do you get if you cross a rabbit with a flea?
Bugs Bunny.

Kent East Brownies

Why is a book like a tree?
Because they both have leaves.

1st Larne Pack

What is the best way to wrap a parcel in an underground room?
Use cellartape.

Breconshire County Pack

In which tree would you hang up your underwear?
In a pantry – or a vestry.

1st Maybole Pack

What did the big telephone say to the little telephone?
You're too young to be engaged.

55th B 'A' Belfast Pack

What can you serve but not eat?
A tennis ball.

Salford Division

Why is tennis a noisy game?
Because every player raises a racket.

2nd Eastbourne Pack

BEAVER BESTSELLERS

You'll find books for everyone to enjoy from Beaver's bestselling range—there are hilarious joke books, gripping reads, wonderful stories, exciting poems and fun activity books. They are available in bookshops or they can be ordered directly from us. Just complete the form below and send the right amount of money and the books will be sent to you at home.

☐	THE ADVENTURES OF KING ROLLO	David McKee	£2.50
☐	MR PINK-WHISTLE STORIES	Enid Blyton	£1.95
☐	FOLK OF THE FARAWAY TREE	Enid Blyton	£1.99
☐	REDWALL	Brian Jacques	£2.95
☐	STRANGERS IN THE HOUSE	Joan Lingard	£1.95
☐	THE RAM OF SWEETRIVER	Colin Dann	£2.50
☐	BAD BOYES	Jim and Duncan Eldridge	£1.95
☐	ANIMAL VERSE	Raymond Wilson	£1.99
☐	A JUMBLE OF JUNGLY JOKES	John Hegarty	£1.50
☐	THE RETURN OF THE ELEPHANT JOKE BOOK	Katie Wales	£1.50
☐	THE REVENGE OF THE BRAIN SHARPENERS	Philip Curtis	£1.50
☐	THE RUNAWAYS	Ruth Thomas	£1.99
☐	EAST OF MIDNIGHT	Tanith Lee	£1.99
☐	THE BARLEY SUGAR GHOST	Hazel Townson	£1.50
☐	CRAZY COOKING	Juliet Bawden	£2.25

If you would like to order books, please send this form, and the money due to:

ARROW BOOKS, BOOKSERVICE BY POST, PO BOX 29, DOUGLAS, ISLE OF MAN, BRITISH ISLES. Please enclose a cheque or postal order made out to Arrow Books Ltd for the amount due including 22p per book for postage and packing both for orders within the UK and for overseas orders.

NAME ....

ADDRESS ....

....

Please print clearly.

Whilst every effort is made to keep prices low it is sometimes necessary to increase cover prices at short notice. Arrow Books reserve the right to show new retail prices on covers which may differ from those previously advertised in the text or elsewhere.